DATE DUE

DEMCO 38-296

MAROON ON GEORGETOWN

NOTES ON PHOTOGRAPHY

All the photographs in this book were taken with Leitz equipment, primarily the Leica single lens reflex system, using R3 and R4 bodies, with lenses ranging from 15mm to 400mm. This was supplemented by Leica M cameras, with lenses from 21mm to 90mm. Exterior scenes were photographed with natural light, using no filters. Interiors were shot with either existing light, or Quartz lights to give the appearance of existing light. Kodachrome was used primarily for exteriors, but also for some interiors. Most interiors were shot with Ektachrome Professional 64 and 50. A tripod and cable release were employed in almost all cases. Kodak laboratories did all the processing.

ACKNOWLEDGMENTS

I am particularly grateful to Jim Weaver and Frank Thomasson; it is largely due to their encouragement that this book was undertaken. To John Grant and his staff I owe an unqualified debt of gratitude for the editing of the photographs, and the superb design of this book. Ross Howell did an equally fine job with text and captions, bringing to the task sensitivity and sound judgement. Charles O. Hyman generously contributed both his time and his extraordinary experience to correcting the color proofs.

Robert Lyle, Joseph Passonneau, Sister Mary Leonard, George Kackley, and Mike Feinstein, all experts in their fields, kindly contributed of their time and information.

Richard Frasier and John Catto gave untiring photographic assistance, and Marc, Anne, Sophia, and Paul Maroon filled in when necessary.

Charlie Rose and Adrian Taylor were the creative forces behind a number of the images.

Sherrie Sandy, as always, was a booster of Georgetown and of this book.

Louis Mercier, my friend and agent in New York, rendered his valuable service and counsel.

This book owes much of its character to the generosity of cooperation of the people whose houses appear in these pages. I am indebted to them all.

Most of all, however, my wife, Suzy, made this book possible by not only organizing all the photographs, but by editing my drafts, and rendering my thoughts and research into the finished text.

Published in 1997 in the United States by Lickle Publishing Inc
590 Madison Avenue, New York, NY 10022

Photographs and text copyright © 1985, 1997 by Fred J. Maroon

Library of Congress Cataloging-in-Publication Data

Maroon, Fred J.
    Maroon on Georgetown / photography and text by Fred J. Maroon. —
  Rev. and enl. ed.
  p. cm.
    ISBN 1-890674-01-X
    1. Georgetown (Washington, D.C.)— Pictorial works. 2. Washington (D.C.) —
  Pictorial works. I. Title. II. Title: Georgetown.
  F202.G3M35   1997
  975.3-DC21   97-17174
                            CIP

Printed In Japan by Toppan Printing Company

MAROON ON
GEORGETOWN

PHOTOGRAPHY AND TEXT BY FRED J. MAROON

LICKLE PUBLISHING INC

CONTENTS

FOREWORD

MY FIRST GLIMPSE OF GEORGETOWN came in 1946, when I was an architectural student at Catholic University, on the other side of Washington. At that time it signified for me little more than the location of Georgetown University, our rival in sports, and our social competition for dates at Trinity College. Three years after graduation, following stints in New York and Paris, I returned to Washington. In 1959 I bought, for reasons of convenience and affordability, a small building on M Street in Georgetown. It was occupied on the ground floor by a Chinese laundry called the Wong Sing, which was almost immediately renamed the "Wrong Thing" by those who had my better interests at heart. My mother, who raised five of us during the Depression in faraway New Jersey, cried when she saw what I had committed myself to. Few people were buying anything on M Street in 1959; it consisted for the most part of secondhand clothing stores, antique shops, pawnshops, and dilapidated, unoccupied reminders of a more prosperous past. Fortunately, there were just enough respectable shops along the street to tip the balance in my favor when I went seeking a bank loan for the purchase and remodeling of the Wong Sing.

Georgetown has not disappointed me. It has given me privacy when I wanted and needed an escape from the physical and emotional pressures that are the occupational hazards of my profession. At the same time it has afforded me as rich a cultural and social life as one could find anywhere in the world. It has given me convenience; any photographic service I might need is only minutes away, and three major airports are not much farther. It has provided me with the research facilities for any project I might undertake. It has been a good place to live. When M Street became too lively and commercial for my young family, we moved a few blocks up the hill to a residential area, but even here I have a delicatessen, a dry cleaner, a convenience store, a liquor store, and a seamstress all within one block of my house. If I venture two blocks afield I can also find a pharmacy, a bookstore, four churches, three public tennis courts, and a large park.

More than anything else, Georgetown has provided me with a photographic set, and a nearly inexhaustible range of subject matter. Over the years my neighbors have often been my subjects: Dean Acheson, Joseph Alsop, Averell Harriman in his home, or Doc Dalinsky with his drugstore full of nationally known personalities. As an architect, I am constantly seeing new things on my strolls through familiar streets. As an incurable romantic, I have felt as much exhilaration at daybreak in Georgetown as I ever did in Karakorum or Connemara. I love to rise before dawn and spend two or three hours photographing in that magical light that the French call "l'heure des anges"—"the hour of the angels." How I relish sitting in my bay window afterwards, watching the rest of the world trudge off to work, as I fortify myself with coffee and croissant!

Georgetown was a natural for a book, and having already authored several on subjects much broader in scope, I naively expected that one about my own backyard would be a snap. I could not have been more mistaken. A project that should have taken a year dragged on for three. Word reached me that people were going into bookstores in search of "the Maroon book on Georgetown," and insisting, in the face of all evidence to the contrary, that such a book existed since "he was working on it years ago." It has been a difficult book to edit; of about 1,000 worthy final candidates, only 101 photographs made it to the printed page. For a number of reasons, this has been the most difficult of all my books to complete.

Firstly, I was working out of my home, and not out of some expensive, inconvenient, unfriendly, or lonely hotel. Between the telephone and the mail, and the daily demands of business, family, and social life, exposing film was often relegated to a back burner. Whereas in Mongolia or Afghanistan I was forever striving to get things done yesterday, on my own home field I was more likely to aim to get them done tomorrow. Invariably, just as tomorrow was about to arrive, an interesting or rewarding assignment would be thrown my way, and tomorrow would become next week, or next month.

Secondly, as soon as I attempted to expand on the images I had collected at random through the years, Georgetown presented obstacles. The trees in summer obscure so much that it is almost impossible to encompass any great areas. Streets are lined with cars year round, and since the original city plans made few provisions for alleys, garbage cans grace the curbs on certain days of the week. It could take all season to find the one day when all the elements were right. Woe to any of my children who were home during dawn or dusk in "weather from heaven" conditions and had let it be known that they had no homework. They were immediately pressed into service as photo assistants, or as they more accurately termed it, pack horses, and we were on our way to a neighborhood I knew would be just right. If a roofer or painter had chosen that day to park his van on my set, the children would hear language not generally tolerated around the house.

Thirdly, there was the problem of setting up a camera in a crowded area like Georgetown. Every other person who passed by was either a friend or, worse, a total stranger interested in photography and wanting to know what I was doing; when it would be coming out; why I was using a tripod; was I sure I had enough light; had I taken a look at so-and-so's house; did I have permission; I should have been here yesterday; what did I think of this or that camera or lens; had I seen the new auto-focus, auto-compose XYZ-7, with a built-in martini dispenser?

Lastly, while I was working on the book, relentless new construction (particularly down by the waterfront) was causing some of my favorite photographs to become outdated. What began as a contemporary look at Georgetown was in constant danger of becoming an historical document. What had been an empty lot was suddenly a building; where the eye had once enjoyed a grand vista, it was now arrested by a solid masonry wall. I rationalize that my procrastination paid off in some ways, as there are a number of new and worthy items in the book that were still on the drawing boards two or three years ago.

Change has been a way of life for Georgetown since its beginning. Today fresh oysters are found in abundance near the banks of the Potomac River, but they are not native; they have been delivered by trucks to the fancy eateries that line the streets. In earlier times, long before Columbus, Algonquin Indians camped in the area at certain times of the year, and loved to feast on the oysters they found in the Potomac. What is now Wisconsin Avenue was then an Indian trail; earlier still it had been a buffalo path leading to the river.

The first recorded European in the area was Captain John Smith. In 1608 he sailed up the Potomac (an Algonquin word which roughly translates as "trading place") in search of gold and a Northwest passage. In 1634 another Englishman, Henry Fleete, wrote of finding "deer, buffalos, bears and turkeys in abundance." At that time an Indian village, Tohoga, existed where Georgetown is now. One of the earliest white settlers in the area was Ninian Beall, a Scot. Beall had fought against Oliver Cromwell, was captured by the British, and subsequently sold into servitude. He arrived in Maryland around 1658 by way of the West Indies, soon earned a reputation in southern Maryland as a great Indian fighter, and by 1672 had begun acquisitions of property that would ultimately make him a major landowner. A part of the parcel of land he called the Rock of Dumbarton is now eastern Georgetown.

Indians had long grown and used tobacco. Colonial planters began to cultivate it in Maryland around 1631. Its immediate popularity in Europe made it the major commodity of exchange for the colonists. The area which is now Georgetown was the furthest navigable reach of the Potomac; Little Falls and Great Falls prevented shipping upriver. As a result, the area developed as an important port. Tobacco was transported down the former Indian trail—Wisconsin Avenue—which now became a "rolling road," and was stored in the tobacco sheds at M Street and Wisconsin Avenue. From there it was shipped directly to England.

By the first half of the 18th century plantation owners in the area were clamoring for a town charter, and after one unsuccessful petition, the Assembly in Annapolis authorized the necessary legislation in 1751. The town, named after George II, was to encompass the properties of George Beall, the son of Ninian, and George Gordon, another Scotsman who owned property adjoining Beall's to the west. Since Gordon also owned the tobacco inspection house on the southwest corner of Wisconsin Avenue and M Street, as well as tobacco sheds, it was to his advantage to have a town chartered where his tobacco interests were centered. He willingly exchanged his land for the proffered 240 pounds and his choice of two lots. George Beall, however, was adamantly opposed, and although he was given the same recompense as Gordon, he remained bitter over the "confiscation" of his property.

The boundaries of early Georgetown were much narrower than those of today. The town extended only from the river up to 120 feet south of N Street, and from 120 feet west of 30th Street on the east to 34th Street on the west. Only one of the original markers remains, in the garden of 1248 30th Street. The town's 60 acres were divided into 80 lots, and its streets were laid out on a grid plan. The lots were put up for sale in March 1752, and 69 were sold at the first offering. Many of them went for one pound ten shillings; some fetched as little as 12½ shillings. The lot on which Riggs Bank now stands, at the corner of M and Wisconsin, sold for four pounds, and the most expensive, Lot No. 40, on the southeast corner of what is now 33rd and M Streets, was purchased by John Lamar for 12 pounds. Buyers had three years in which to erect a "substantial house with a chimney." Of the original buildings erected, only the Old Stone House, begun in 1764 on Lot No. 3 on M Street, remains to give us an idea of what the original buildings may have looked like.

Georgetown grew rapidly and its boundaries soon became inadequate. "Additions" of adjacent parcels of land were annexed and named after their owners. The first, the Beatty and Hawkins Addition, was in 1769, and in 1783 and 1785 further additions of land belonging to Thomas Beall, grandson of Ninian, were made. A large baronial house constructed about 1780 by Thomas' brother, George Beall, stood on one of these additions, and may still be seen at 3033 N Street.

In the first two decades of the 19th century Georgetown prospered as a port. Although Bridge Street (now M Street) was always the commercial center of Georgetown, Water Street (now K Street) bustled with warehouses and taverns for seamen. There was a small influx of Northerners into Georgetown during this time. Some of the newcomers were sailors and sea captains from Salem, Massachusetts, who were involved in the West India trade and were probably looking for a good ice-free port out of which to operate. Among them was Francis Dodge, who was to become the owner of a large shipping firm, and eventually the wealthiest man in Georgetown. Unfortunately for him, the river began to silt up in the 1820s. Ships were becoming larger, and those utilizing steam required a deeper channel. Georgetown ceased to be a viable port, and when the Crash of 1857 hit shipping especially hard, the F. and A.H. Dodge firm went under. Two of Dodge's sons had engaged the highly respected Philadelphia architectural firm, Downing and Vaux, to design grandiose houses for them; Robert, who was not involved in shipping, was able to move into his mansion at 1534 28th Street, but Francis, his brother, eventually lost the mirror-image house he was building at 1537 30th Street. The two houses still stand, although the one on 28th Street was extensively remodeled in the 1950s. Some imagination is required to detect the similarity between them now.

The city commissioners, recognizing that Georgetown's days of prosperity as a port were numbered, tried to generate other commercial interest in the area. Hopes were pinned on the Chesapeake and Ohio Canal, which was begun in 1828 and was to serve as the trade route between the Ohio River settlements and the Chesapeake Bay area. It was never finished, extending only as far west as Cumberland, Maryland, but its eastern terminus was Georgetown. Although it did not become the financial bonanza the commissioners envisioned, the C & O Canal did bring a measure of commercial success. It allowed coal, limestone, wheat, produce, and lumber to be brought down to Georgetown, and provided water power for the mills that grew up alongside it.

The Civil War was a wrenching period in the history of Georgetown. Situated on the border between North and South, Georgetown had its share of Southern sympathizers as well as abolitionists. When their men put on Confederate uniforms and went off to war, some of the women left behind became spies for the Confederacy, relaying decisions as fast as the Union generals made them. The Battle of Bull Run was won on such intelligence. Holy Trinity Church was used as a hospital by the Union Army, and wounded soldiers from both sides were brought to Georgetown Visitation Convent for care. Nuns from both the North and the South were in residence at the convent, and the archbishop ordered that the war not be discussed, as it only brought on trouble between the two sides. When the wounded were brought in, they were discreetly assigned to nuns with similar sympathies.

The end of the Civil War ushered in a period of prosperity for Georgetown. In 1871 the city lost its charter and became an integral part of the District of Columbia. Streets lost their former picturesque names—Gay Street, Duck Lane, Water Street, Fishing Lane—in favor of the more practical, but much less poetic, letters and numbers of Washington's grid system. From 1880 to 1900 more houses were built in Georgetown than at any other time; perhaps as many as half the houses in Georgetown are built in this late Victorian, or Queen Anne style, which was characterized by intricate and ornate brickwork. The houses built during this time ranged from grand and elaborate mansions on the north side of town, to tiny mill-hand and blue-collar houses south of M Street. Georgetown was home to people from all walks of life.

As World War I approached, changes were afoot. In 1915 Robert Todd Lincoln purchased and redid an enormous house at 3014 N Street. Robert Woods Bliss bought Dumbarton Oaks in 1920 and practically reconstructed it, inside and out. In 1923 Ferdinand Lammot Belin acquired and redid Evermay. During the 1920s all the fine old Federal houses in Georgetown were bought up, quite cheaply, and redone. When Franklin Roosevelt became president in 1932, large numbers of political aides accompanied him; they too discovered the ambience and convenience of Georgetown, and the buying mania spread to other houses. Gas rationing in World War II sent Georgetown's stock even higher. After the war houses that had been built for $1,000 were sold for $50,000.

Fortunately, in 1950 the Old Georgetown Act was passed, declaring Georgetown a National Landmark and designating as its permanent boundaries Rock Creek Park, the Potomac River, Dumbarton Oaks Park, and Glover-Archbold Parkway. The act ensured the survival, intact, of the residential section of Georgetown. It did not alter the existing zoning of the industrial area south of M Street, however, which included the C & O Canal. Until recently the area contained lumber yards, a sand and gravel works, a flour mill, and a rendering plant that emitted such distinctive odors that the flour mill next door felt compelled to post a large sign, disclaiming responsibility! The Whitehurst Freeway was constructed in 1949 over K Street, right along the banks of the Potomac. Built to relieve traffic congestion on M Street, it was considered a blessing at the time. Georgetown's historic waterfront, however, was hidden and its future compromised by this utilitarian, elevated four-lane expressway. For years the freeway has inhibited the natural development of Georgetown toward the river, and prevented a waterfront renaissance which the exquisite location deserves. Recently, however, the industrial structures in the area have been taken over by developers and often imaginatively redesigned as office buildings, chic shops, apartments, hotels, and restaurants.

Now my peaceful little community has become a major urban settlement, while retaining much of its small-town residential charm. For some people Georgetown is little more than a commuters' alley, a logjam of traffic trying to escape out Wisconsin Avenue or Canal Road to Maryland, or across Key Bridge to Virginia. For tourists who invade from spring to fall it is a place to touch base with history, and to gawk at the houses of the rich and famous. For students at Georgetown University it is both campus and playground. And for all it is an urban boardwalk, a place to see and be seen, by day and by night. There are shops for every taste, from Sunny's Surplus to Abercrombie & Fitch, from Commander Salamander to Britches. Restaurants cater to any appetite and pocketbook, from a Little Tavern (old enough to be acceptable) and a Burger King (newly opened, and decidedly unacceptable to many residents), to the Four Seasons and the 1789. One can find cuisine from China and Argentina, and most places in between. Galleries and antique shops abound for both collector and browser. For the young and energetic there are music and dancing; for the more sedentary there are over a dozen movie houses. Exclusive clubs exist for those who prefer more private entertainment.

In the last few years Georgetown has emerged as the stage upon which people from Washington and its suburbs gather to act out their triumphs and frustrations. Pennsylvania Avenue may be the capital's official parade route, but the emotional heartbeat of the city is more strongly felt in Georgetown. When Charlie Brown's final touchdown followed John Riggins' spectacular run in Super Bowl XVII, the game clock had barely run out in Los Angeles before the horns were blaring along every approach to Georgetown; within an hour thousands of fans had converged on Wisconsin Avenue and M Street in a spontaneous display of elation at their 'Skins' achievement. On Halloween night it has become a tradition for Georgetown to be turned into a parade route for trick-or-treaters of all ages; it is Georgetown's own brand of Mardi Gras.

Certainly Georgetown residents of earlier generations would not approve of everything that has been done here, and yet they created the framework upon which this unique living monument has evolved. Within each period there have been those who have been steadfastly opposed to change, and those who have been equally firmly devoted to changes which they perceived to be for the better. In Georgetown these two forces seem, for the most part, to have struck a harmonious balance. Each generation has had its own set of circumstances, and each has left its mark on the village. It is not the same Georgetown I moved into 25 years ago, and yet I feel that what is being passed on to those who follow is both a living legacy and a challenge.

Georgetown Residential

FRIENDS VISITING FROM ABROAD invariably comment that Georgetown is unlike other American cities—it reminds them of Europe. Certainly the Federal houses built here, and in cities up and down the East Coast, were directly influenced by the Georgian architecture of England. Later this gave way to the Victorian and Queen Anne styles; the majority of houses in Georgetown were built during the second half of the 19th century. These too are typical of structures built in other American cities at the time. Yet nowhere else in the country has an entire historic town been preserved more or less intact, within a major city, as has been the case here. Even after Georgetown became an integral part of Washington, its residents fought vigorously to preserve its character and charm. Without their effort, the history of Georgetown might have been quite different.

Many Georgetown houses, both Federal and Victorian, were built from builders' pattern books which contained a variety of floor plans and details. Often houses were built on speculation; the typical method was to build three alike, live in one, and sell or rent the other two. Also popular was the double house, two identical houses, attached to look like one, and built on four lots. The style was very common in England and France; it had a certain grandeur, and allowed light and a garden on three sides of each house. Throughout Georgetown are a number of superb mansions built by the leading architects of various periods.

The interesting thing about Georgetown houses is that they remain constant even in change. They are always being brought up to date, and many have been remodeled two or three times. However, the external appearance of most has not changed much. Indeed, since 1950, any projected alterations to the exteriors of existing houses must pass the Georgetown Board of Review and the Fine Arts Commission. The few new houses being built are required to conform to standards harmonious with Georgetown's historic character. Somewhat greater latitude is permitted in areas which are not visible from public streets.

The interior of a Georgetowner's house, however, is his castle. Anything goes, from lovingly tasteful preservations of another era's elegance to starkly contemporary urban living. The often unpretentious facade of a house serves to heighten the surprise at what awaits within, and in dealing with the limitations imposed by the size of the existing structure, some architects have produced wonderfully imaginative and dramatic use of space.

Why do people choose to live in Georgetown? When Washington was being built, Georgetown offered the only good housing in the area for members of Congress; a stagecoach shuttled them back and forth to the Capitol. Now people live here for the same reasons: convenience and quality of life. Capitol Hill is only three miles distant, and much of commercial and professional Washington lies between it and Georgetown. Just one block away from the frenetic commercial hubs of Wisconsin Avenue and M Street, an entirely different world exists. It is a world with human scale, a world—rare in America—that is not dependent on the automobile, where most of one's daily needs, and a good many friends and dinner parties, are within walking distance.

Who chooses to live here? Blacks and whites, old and young. Americans, of course, but there is always a sizable contingent of foreigners, who possibly feel more at home here than they would in the suburbs. The anonymous and the famous; Georgetown has been home to Henry Kissinger and Elizabeth Taylor, John Kennedy and many of his relatives. A stroll or errand could bring one face to face with Averell Harriman, Katharine Graham, Herman Wouk, or Senator Charles Percy.

Georgetown is not without its flaws, and those of us who live here are only too well aware of them. But it has more than enough unique and diverse qualities to tip the balance in its favor. If I didn't live here, I would want to.

DUMBARTON OAKS

ON THE NORTHERN EDGE OF GEORGETOWN stands Dumbarton Oaks, a Georgian mansion in a 16-acre country estate which has been described as "America's most civilized square mile." In the house is the Dumbarton Oaks Center for Byzantine Studies, operated by Harvard University, which is the largest library in the world devoted solely to Byzantium. Attached to the mansion is the small but exquisite Byzantine Museum. These owe their existence to the last owners of the house, Mr. and Mrs. Robert Woods Bliss. Mr. Bliss' postings in the foreign service permitted them to indulge their mania for collecting and their fascination with the Middle Ages. The carefully assembled collection of Byzantine art provided the foundation for a major world center for Byzantine studies. Also at Dumbarton Oaks, in a small jewel of a gallery designed by Philip Johnson, is an important collection of pre-Columbian art. This was primarily the passion of Mr. Bliss, who attended an exhibition of pre-Columbian works in Paris in 1912, and continued to collect from that day until his death in 1962. Another addition to the property houses the Garden Library, a repository of more than 11,500 books, many of them rare, on the history of landscape architecture. This was the work of the indefatigable Mrs. Bliss.

The glorious Music Room at Dumbarton Oaks has provided a stage for some of the world's greatest musicians for over half a century. Igor Stravinsky's "Dumbarton Oaks Concerto," commissioned by Mrs. Bliss as an anniversary present for her husband, was given its premiere there in 1938. Stravinsky himself conducted in the room, and other artists who have performed there include Nadia Boulanger, François Poulenc, Aaron Copland, Joan Sutherland, Samuel Barber, Leontyne Price, and Dietrich Fischer-Dieskau. In 1944 two international conferences were held in the Music Room to draft principles which were later incorporated in the Charter of the United Nations.

Surrounding the mansion, the most magnificent formal gardens in Washington provide a romantic intermission for the poet in us during any season of the year. I have often encountered a friend out for a solitary stroll on one of the terraces in the dead of winter. Spring brings flowers and visitors in abundance, and while summer cannot compete with the extraordinary colors of its predecessor, it still offers relief from Washington's infamous heat and humidity. Fall is a farewell, as the magnificent autumnal colors make a last stand before their winter rest. The garden is the creation of Mrs. Bliss and her landscape gardener, Beatrix Jones Farrand, who was a great admirer of English gardens. The two women worked together for more than a quarter of a century, sparing no effort to ensure perfection of detail. Architectural features are intricately incorporated with the planting, each complementing the other. The terraces that recede from the house are individual, self-contained gardens, designed with variety, harmony, and balance.

Adjoining the cultivated gardens are 27 acres of the original estate, which were donated to the nation by Mr. and Mrs. Bliss, and form one of America's least known wilderness areas—Dumbarton Oaks Park. This is entered from R Street, by way of Lover's Lane.

The land on which Dumbarton Oaks stands was originally part of the holdings of Ninian Beall. The estate was known as the Rock of Dumbarton, named after a famous rock on the Clyde in Beall's native Scotland. A Federal-style house, the first on the site, was constructed around 1800 by William Hammond Dorsey. The house was changed in character during the course of the 19th century by several owners. In 1920 the greater part of the estate was purchased by Mr. and Mrs. Bliss, who completely remodeled the house and named it Dumbarton Oaks. In 1940 they gave Dumbarton Oaks to Harvard University, Mr. Bliss' alma mater, that "the continuity of scholarship in Byzantine and Mediaeval humanities may remain unbroken."

GEORGETOWN UNIVERSITY

TO MOST PEOPLE OUTSIDE WASHINGTON, "Georgetown" means Georgetown University. Founded at the time that Washington was named the nation's capital, the university is the oldest Catholic and Jesuit institution of higher education in the U.S. Its founder was John Carroll, first bishop of the American Catholic Church, brother to a signer of the Constitution, and friend of George Washington. A Jesuit who had been educated in Europe, Bishop Carroll perceived the need for an institution which, while based on the traditional concepts of St. Ignatius of Loyola, would be an American institution, serving the needs of the developing nation and open to those of all religious faiths. With financial backing from the Catholic clergy and Catholics in England and America, Bishop Carroll purchased for 75 pounds one and a half acres "at George Town on the Potowmack" for an "Academy." Construction began, and in 1789 Georgetown College was established.

Georgetown's first student arrived in November 1791. By the end of the 18th century the school consisted of two buildings, Old South and Old North, surrounded by meadows, orchards, and woodlands. Old North, completed in 1791, was visited by George Washington and still stands.

The fortunes of the young school were insecure. In 1806 enrollment had fallen to 34 students, and there was talk of moving the school to New York. Washington was perceived as a backwater, whereas New York was flourishing. The judgment of Bishop Carroll, who envisioned Washington one day becoming a world capital, prevailed; the school remained in Georgetown. Not long after, when the British invaded Washington in 1814 and burned the White House, one observer wrote that the flames were so bright that it was possible to read by their light at the college, more than two miles away.

The Civil War came close to destroying Georgetown. Students, especially Southerners, began to leave campus. Soldiers of the New York Militia's 69th (Irish) Regiment were billeted in students' quarters for a few months in the early part of the war; students had to double up to make room for them. Later the Army Medical Corps took over some of the university's facilities for the care of the wounded. At the end of the war, the university made a gesture of healing and unity by adopting blue and gray as the school's colors.

The task of rebuilding Georgetown after the Civil War fell to Father Patrick Healy, often referred to as Georgetown's second founder. It was he who set the course for Georgetown to grow from a small college into a major university. He also undertook the university's largest building project to date: the Flemish Romanesque stone building which bears his name (against his modest wishes) and which has dominated the Georgetown skyline since 1879.

Until recently, the university never had enough dormitory space, and students have lived in rooms and houses throughout town. At one time, leaving the grounds of the university without permission meant suspension or even expulsion, and there are undoubtedly Georgetown residents who, around two on a weekend morning, wish that rule were still in effect. In truth, however, the university is an immensely valuable resource, offering lectures, concerts, libraries, and evening courses to those who wish to take advantage of them. And in May, when cars have been loaded and students have left, there may be more parking spaces on the streets, but there is also a sense of something missing: the vitality, enthusiasm, playfulness, and optimism that keep us young. For those graduating, this rite of passage is summed up in the "Cohonguroton Oration," the college's valedictory address. Cohonguroton means "River of Swans," and is the oldest known Indian name for the Potomac. It is a fitting name for a swansong.

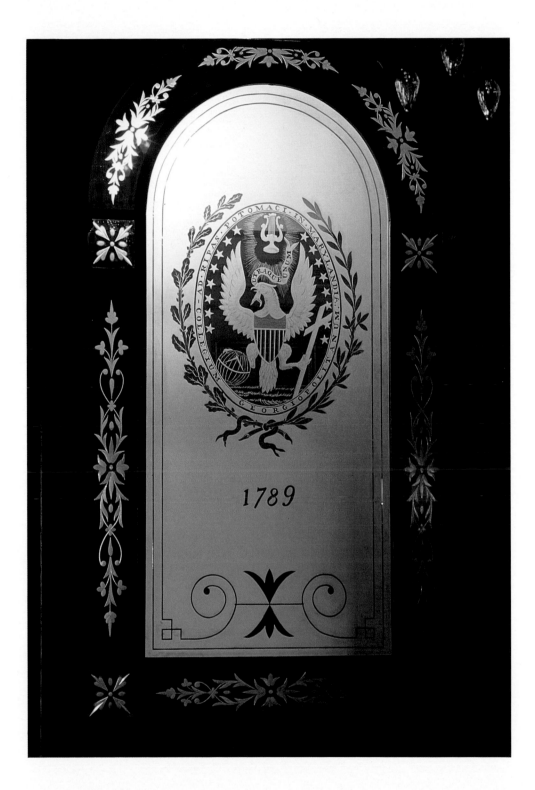

135

NOTES ON THE PHOTOGRAPHY

ONE OF THE FOUR AMERICAN BISONS GUARDING THE ENDS OF DUMBARTON BRIDGE. Sculpted by A. Phimister Proctor in 1913, they are the reason for the bridge's affectionate, if mistaken, nickname: the Buffalo Bridge. It crosses Rock Creek Park on Q Street, at the eastern edge of Georgetown.

39

EVERMAY. The Georgian-style manor house was built in 1801 for Samuel Davidson, a Georgetown merchant and land developer. Davidson owned much of the land on which the federal city would eventually be built, including that where the White House now stands. The house was designed by Nicholas King, from Yorkshire, England, who was working as a surveyor during the planning of Washington. Evermay was restored in 1923 by F. Lammot Belin, who removed some Victorian accretions to the house. Situated on a hill at the northeastern edge of Georgetown, it is surrounded by almost four acres of landscaped gardens, which feature a profusion of trees, shrubs, and flowers, a Georgian-style temple, and a Chinese-style pavilion.

40

A STATUE IN THE GARDEN AT EVERMAY.

41

TUDOR PLACE. The Federal period mansion was designed by Dr. William Thornton, the first architect of the United States Capitol, for Martha Custis Peter, the granddaughter of Martha Washington. With her husband, Mrs. Peter purchased the entire city block for $8,000 — her legacy from George Washington. The house was completed in 1816, and is surrounded by acres of lawns, specimen trees and formal gardens. Among the illustrious visitors to the house were the Marquis de Lafayette, Daniel Webster, John C. Calhoun, and Robert E. Lee. It remained in the Custis-Peter family until 1984, and is a National Historic Landmark, owned and operated by Tudor Place Foundation, Inc.

42-43

CORNER, 28TH AND Q STREET. An incurable romantic like me finds it hard to get to sleep in Georgetown during a snowstorm. At 2 a.m. in the middle of the blizzard of 1966 very few cars or people intruded on my set.

45

3038 N STREET. Built by Romulus Riggs of the Riggs banking family about 1812, the house was later owned by Averell and Pamela Harriman. It was at Averell Harriman's invitation that Jacqueline Kennedy moved here from the White House immediately after the assassination of her husband. She later purchased a house across the street before finally moving to New York.

46

2800 BLOCK, N STREET. The block, built around 1812-13, is one of the most beautiful rows of Federal brick houses in Georgetown.

47

BRASS DOOR KNOCKER. This elegant dolphin knocker is similar to those seen on the palaces and grand houses on the island of Malta, where it is considered to be a symbol of good luck. Georgetown door knockers are as varied and imaginative as the personalities behind the doors.

48-53

THE JOHN STODDERT HAW HOUSE, N STREET. (p.48) Entrance hall. The interior arch and fan light are particularly fine features of this Federal house. The house escaped the Victorian alterations that were the fate of many other houses of this period. (p.49) Portrait of the wife of the present owner of the house done by Charles Childs c. 1945. The portrait hangs over one of two exquisite mantels in the living area of the house. (p.50) Corner detail of a mirror above a mantel in the living room, and a Central American mask, probably Mayan. (p.51) Jade bowl filled with jade and amethyst fruit, and other objects, in the living room. (p.52) Under a corner lamp in the living room, a celadon bowl (Chinese porcelain), a quartz bowl, and presentation portraits collected by the present owners of the house. (p.53) Terra cotta figurines from Tanagra, Greece.

54-57

THE HOUSE OF THE LATE SECRETARY OF STATE MR. AND MRS. DEAN ACHESON, P STREET. (p.54) The American flag in the corner belonged to her husband while he was with the State Department. Over the mantel is a painting by Mrs. Acheson, c. 1945, of the Maryland countryside near their farm. (p.55) Desk used by Mr. Acheson in his study. (p.56) Portrait of Mrs. Acheson by Alexander James, painted c. 1950. The portrait hangs in the drawing room of a wing added by the Achesons in 1928. Alexander James was the son of the philosopher, William James. Beneath the painting are the 19th century miniature portraits of the maternal grandparents of Mr. Acheson (left) and Mrs. Acheson (right). The needlepoint on the sofa was done by Mrs. Acheson's granddaughter when she was 12 years old. (p.57) A silver platter in the dining room bears the inscription: "The Honorable Dean Acheson from the Chiefs of Mission in Washington, in Token of Their Appreciation and High Regard. January 1953."

58

1200 BLOCK, 30TH STREET. These 19th century residences are beautifully restored and preserved.

59

PRIVATE COLLECTION. The often eclectic collections of Georgetown residents reflect their tastes and interests.

60-63

THE HOUSE OF MR. BENJAMIN C. BRADLEE. Mr. Bradlee, former Executive Editor of *The Washington Post*, and his wife, Sally Quinn, live in this house built by shipping merchant John Laird in 1797. (p.60) Central staircase. Robert Todd Lincoln, the eldest son of the president, purchased the house in 1918. (p.61) Dining room. The Canton china (foreground) belonged to Mr. Bradlee's ancestors. The sideboard has been in the family since the 19th century. The dining room and kitchen (visible in the mirror) were added onto the original house in the 19th century. (pp.62-63) Living room, decorated by Mrs. Bradlee. In the original house this was two rooms; they were combined in 1978 by the former owner. In the center of the room is a 19th century Chinese mourning screen. Over the mirror on the left is a painting by Leon Dabo. Over the right mantel is a painting by the 19th century American Impressionist Allen Tucker.

64-65

THE HOUSE OF MR. AND MRS. HUGH N. JACOBSEN. Mr. Jacobsen is an internationally respected architect who lives and works in Georgetown. (p.64) Living room. The painting on the left is "Homage to the Square: Astonish" by Josef Albers, c. 1962. On the right is "Arundel" by Anne Truitt, 1980. A portion of Mr. Jacobsen's library is visible beyond the Italian sofa. (p.65) Floor-to-ceiling egg-crate bookcase. The bookcase is a trademark of Mr. Jacobsen's architecture. The library, just off the house's garden, is part of a 1968 addition.

66-69

FORMERLY THE STAR CARPET WORKS. In remodeling this building in 1979, architect Arthur Cotton Moore essentially situated a residence within the walls of a 1930 carpet-cleaner factory, rather like putting a ship in a bottle. (pp.66-67) The old factory had textured terra cotta walls, which were retained like a castle enclosure, creating a contrast with the soft, high-tech structure within. The internal courtyard contains a lap pool in the shape of an unfolding rug. Moore describes the house as "an urban castle that seems machine perfect." (p.66) From the Plexiglass bubble in the living room a curved-glass, tube-like gallery on the right leads to the rear pavilion, containing the maid's and children's rooms, and sauna for the pool. (p.68) The staircase looks out to the step-down living room and French doors to the balcony. (p.69) Corkscrew staircase at the entrance. At the right is a gallery leading to the living room.

70-73

THE HOUSE OF MR. AND MRS. WARREN COX. It is one of three houses built c. 1875 in the 3100 block, N Street. Mr. Cox is one of Washington's leading architects. His 1972 restoration of the house followed two prior remodelings that opened up the living room to the dining room and added about seven feet to the house. (p.70) Beyond the light-box coffee table in the foreground, three arches demarcate the living room, library-sitting area, and dining room. (p.71) In the living room a circular opening into the hall frames a 1971 painting by Lowell Nesbitt entitled, "Diana Staircase." A picture rail supports three pencil and ink drawings. (pp.72-73) Below the curved dropped ceiling of the dining room hang 18th century Piranesi engravings (left). The living room is in the background. (p.73) The table settings are English Sheffield Regency silver. Behind is an 18th century American chest, with a toy car from the 1930s.

74-75

THE HOUSE OF MR. AND MRS. HUNTINGTON BLOCK, 30TH STREET. The house was built in 1868 as part of a double house, and was remodeled in 1968 by Arthur Cotton Moore. Mr. Moore changed the house dramatically; the entrance was moved from the front of the house to the side (just visible on the left of the photograph), creating an entrance hall in the center of the house off the garden. The entire floor plan was altered, and a dining room (visible at the end of the corridor) was added to the rear of the house. The Indian elephant was bought by Mr. Block at a charity auction. (p.75) In the dining room is a painting of 15-year-old America Burche, an ancestress of Mrs. Block who was educated in a female seminary and was offered the first presidency of a women's college in Kentucky. Below the portrait is a Chinese rose medallion pattern bowl.

76-79

THE CORNER OF 31ST AND P STREETS. The house was built by J. Edward Libby, a wealthy lumber merchant, in 1876. During John F. Kennedy's inauguration in 1961 the owners, Admiral and Mrs. Neill Phillips, turned it over for use as a guest house by the Kennedys; Mr. and Mrs. Joseph P. Kennedy stayed here. (p.78) Objects collected by the families of other former owners include (left to right) a presentation cane, a gift from Joseph Pulitzer; a silver presentation cup, c. 1870; a silver horse; and a pair of mother-of-pearl-covered Tiffany binoculars. (p.79) The place setting includes a Wedgwood plate and Tiffany silver from the turn of the century.

136-137
THE FORMER FRENCH MARKET, WISCONSIN AVENUE.

138-139
LOWER WISCONSIN AVENUE. Behind the shops and restaurants can be seen some remodeled mills and warehouses and new office buildings. In the background are the Washington Monument, the Watergate complex, and the John F. Kennedy Center for the Performing Arts.

139
GEORGETOWN PHARMACY, WISCONSIN AVENUE. Better known as "Doc Dalinsky's," the Georgetown Pharmacy was for years been an informal gathering spot for some of Washington's most celebrated figures. Pictured are (left to right) David Brinkley, Doc Dalinsky, Ben Bradlee, and Art Buchwald.

140
BARNES & NOBLE BOOKSELLERS, AND EDDIE BAUER, ON M STREET.

141
GARDEN ROOM OF THE GEORGETOWN CLUB. This elegant city club was founded in 1966.

142
THE ARBOR ROOM. This private dining room is in the Four Seasons Hotel, at the entrance to Georgetown on Pennsylvania Avenue.

143
RICHARD McCOOEY, FOUNDER OF THE 1789 RESTAURANT. Near Georgetown University, the restaurant takes its name from the year of the university's founding. Together with its nightclub neighbor, F. Scott's, 1789 attracts a wide circle of clientele, including Georgetown alumni who have made good. Georgetown students, on the other hand, prefer the ambience of the Tombs, in the basement of the building.

144
M STREET, LOOKING TOWARD GEORGETOWN UNIVERSITY.

145
WEATHERVANE AND CUPOLA, CRESTAR BANK, M STREET.

146
A DECORATIVE WINDOW FRAME.

147
LOOKING WEST ON M STREET AT SUNSET.

148
HOLY SATURDAY MASS AT HOLY TRINITY CHURCH. The parish was founded in 1790. The first church for the parish was constructed in 1792. Now serving as Holy Trinity Convent, it stands at 3513 N Street, and is the oldest church building in Washington. In 1849 the cornerstone for a larger church was laid next door to the original building to accommodate the rapidly growing Catholic population of Georgetown. The present interior dates from 1979. President Kennedy worshipped here as a senator and as president, and attended Mass here for the last time the Sunday before his assassination in 1963.

149-151
OAK HILL CEMETERY, R STREET. (p.149) Built in 1850, the cemetery chapel was designed by James Renwick, who also designed the Renwick Gallery (formerly the Corcoran Gallery of Art) near the White House. His work for the chapel was commissioned by William Wilson Corcoran, a successful Washington businessman. Oak Hill Cemetery was Corcoran's gift to Washington, and his first major philanthropy. (p.120) Detail of the black iron fence on the R Street side of Oak Hill Cemetery. The work of Jacob Bigelow from Harvard, the fence and its gates were done in an Egyptian style. (pp.150-151) Oak Hill Cemetery was designed by George F. de la Roche as a garden cemetery, and is the major burial ground in Georgetown. Some stones actually predate the cemetery, and were moved to it at a later time. Oak Hill is one of a series of great garden cemeteries built around America in the middle of the last century.

152-153
THE POTOMAC RIVER AND FRANCIS SCOTT KEY BRIDGE AT SUNSET.

154
ANONYMOUS BUST, RIGGS MEMORIAL LIBRARY, GEORGETOWN UNIVERSITY.

160
ROWBOATS, C & O CANAL.

GEORGETOWN

Georgetown University

Dumbarton Oaks

Oak Hill Cemetery

early Georgetown

Potomac River

Map courtesy of Joseph R. Passonneau